*Poetic Alcoholic*

*It begins here, with you.*

# Poetic Alcoholic

*Hasan J. Syed*

There are no contents, your heart belongs here with those new tears; I shall paint you and blossom you into the beautiful flowers you are.

Please open your heart and those places in your mind where the seeds of unjust torture sit and are waiting to be freed.

*Dedicated to my best friend, Sef Khan*
*Thank you for all the memories of the countless nights in the city where we laughed our asses off in the subway and dinners where you inspired me through conversations to make some beautiful works.*

*All the love.*

These are words of wisdom that came from the places where people's hearts grew cold and where they lost their innocence. The part where each one of them became better at goodbyes and the word "sorrows" became a melody of unbreached silence. After all the chaos these words were tears that became dry.

Everyone asks me where these poems and such sacred pain comes from; happy to tell you that "you" are the reason why these words exist, why your pain and tears bleed to form all these beautiful texts that relate to your beautiful misery. You have realised your deepest fears in this piece of literature that forms such caves of honey that you obtain the heart that you wish was yours. It sounds painful and I sound kind of a psychopath but the truth is you'll read these texts and hope that some palaces were never meant to be made and the beauty that was captivated by the remorse of humanity are pigmented on these pages of misery yet some are happy but those were a tragic happiness. But in some scenarios, there was happiness that I captured from you people; "Happiness" that I caught from individuals who grew on me over the days and kept some notions of their endearing politeness, ones that held so much hope and glistened by their personalities that chose to live and not die over some ill infatuation. You created beautiful poems that brought out the beauty in me that I never knew existed.

*This is the collection of some of my finest work and some random thoughts I wrote down on my travels. These words have been through several countries, train rides and some intoxication that brought new passages and portals to new dimensions of my brain. Honestly there were many times where Sef and I would be on the train and walking through the city where we would improv the shit out of scenarios we imagined or just added on to lines of films that we love especially every conversation between Professor X and Magneto. You realise through all the times when you are around such people how every being carries such literature that creates such forms of art that glorifies you in ways that you want to drown in that piece of creation temporary. I don't know what to tell you but all of this has been such a journey where countless nights I have dreamed for this moment to finish these texts for you. A lot people asked me if any of these poems are about me so let me tell you something; yes, some of them are about myself but mostly are about others and the beauty they have given this book. There are some poems where you'll know right off the back that these are about some of my ordeals. I have set these texts raw and untouched from my mind to this canvas, nothing was thought about, it was all written with my eyes closed to the voices in my mind and melodies to such beautiful people like you.*

*There are people like you and I that lay awake on sleepless nights battling with the voices and demons in our minds. And these pieces are the thoughts and battles for you and I, where the sea deepens and people no longer swim in the shallows. There are those who meet me and question who I am and where I came from, questioning my purges and what I hold in the paradox of me or the mystery of me; with that being said, here is a part of my mind.*

*Thank you for your patience with me through your love and support you have given me, I hope this heals your wounds and your scars that you are scared to show; you are the beauty why my poems exist.*

*Man was intoxicated in your smiles and glistening aura.*

*You gave him the chance that he would fly to Eden and steal all the flowers under God where he was placed in hell for you.*

**He'll never be with you**

*Maybe jealousy was a fuel that burned your sins as you committed more murder.*

*You ate me raw and ripped me bit by bit*

*I loved you even then.*

*I wonder how many nights it would take to kill you? Days, months or years?*

*It took one night where you spilled your love for me and where I stood and said*

"You're looking for the wrong love for I saw it in your eyes of how fragile you were and all I ever wanted to do was break you."

*I woke in the midst of angels that stood with brooms and mops that cleaned my blood and tar.*

**"You came here with her but you didn't realise her wings were clipped from her for she killed them all and burned the kingdom of Eden that once stood."**

*I know your love was a sword to my heart*

*He may hold love that is more golden than mine. But don't forget that love is delusional. He may lay you in shapes and ways I couldn't before.*

*Maybe that wasn't how my love was intended, it was pure not toxic.*

***I heard the voices of the demons calling***

***And I sat down looking for Mecca and I found the voices of angels chanting my name saying,***

*"Oh indeed God calls upon you and says you have been bestowed by blessings that your mother has prayed for"*

*You indulged me into sheets and poison that had me screaming for you.*

*Your rich honey coated tongue that tasted every inch of me fouled and fuelled my lust for you.*

*I wanted you to destroy me in ways you hadn't before in your own demise to purify me*

**Love me where your soul bleeds.**

*You scraped at my soul to find my last ounces of love*

*But I was there to drain you out of the blood and tears you took from me*

*Love is beautiful; so is death.*

***I sung right beside you.***

*You laid there, bleeding and gasping for breath. I fell in love with you again, I feasted on your blood that gave ink to my brushes to imprison more like you.*

***Tell me you love me and I'll make it easy.***

*All those countless nights where we yelled
times where you hit with the pain of your tears*

*crying on my chest while I couldn't hold you*

*my anger was unjust through the fragile eyes that loved me*

*His touches on your skin that feel unjust and cold
he holds you tight yet so fragilely*

*I know you've been hurt and broken before*

*he sees paradise in you, don't lose faith*

**You** remind me of flowers.

You hold the scents of Eden and when you smile; the fragile dusk smiles amidst the night with beauties that astound man.

You make man climb to the moon and bring you the stars

What am I to you?

You are the moon that fills the darkness with light but even that darkness is an illusion for I have died countlessly for you to shine.

A false accusation of love that you called soul binding.

*What do you love she asked?*

*I love you for you are broken in ways that can't be broken more but I promise you*

*I will break you more till the blood runs down your cheeks that wish for your death*

*Sex was an ordeal that stitched legs and arms that entitled deeds of Paradise?*

*No, it was in the car where he ripped me and I cried inside but I was so excited but it wasn't who I was, it was him that shredded me and left in matters of seconds*

*You asked me what love was.*

*Simply it was you in the form of weary dry eyes and where your throat suffocated from the looks of unloving eyes*

*What was the greatest lesson I learned about you?*

*You were nothing but illusion and I thought I loved you but now that I think about the taste of your lips*

*I am disgusted in the ordeals I kept with you*

*Your rose petals were soft and filled with scents
that reminded me of what heaven could be*

*but you were all the right reasons why I fell in your oceans
of pureness*

*I woke up in the midst of your blood tainted in across my body*

*You laid there;*
*eyes open and your heart open for love that never existed*

*The honey that seeps from your lips that quenches my thirst for a canvas that glistens with colours that an artist like me lusts for.*

*Tell me how to win your heart*

*Her lips lingered with sweetness that numbed my pain; her outline was one that reminded me of the banks of Paradise*

*And there she stood still as a silent mortar to the battlefields of love; she was paradise to the endless nights of misery where I held her close.*

*She was pure and she had me intoxicated*

*The blood that rushed down your body, the white sheets that once presented the gardens of God were now red to the colour of your love*

*Now tainted to my weary soul; I looked at you as you shivered from the cold that was here to take your soul*

*I stood there; smiling and licking my lips that were stained of your blood.*

*You've earned it.*

*She caressed art as critics would; she would find the directions from the strokes of dry weary paint that glistened colours in form of heavy strokes. She would find feelings that would carve out ways that touched her demons that laid awake in her soul.*

*She was a critic to her own demise, where the world viewed her as art and where she wiped the ink that dripped from veins onto her own canvas to paint herself into heavier strokes that she questioned if it was enough*

*You loved her like a vessel of pleasure; she became immune to the needles of your lustful fingers*

*your skin that smelled like cinnamon was a piece that she wanted*

*her broken shallow heart became your whiskey glass that you drained life out of*

*Poetic Alcoholic*

*Trapped in four walls that burned my eyes like catholic confessions; Sundays had become days at mass where I would drink out of my flask*

*your name was engraved in my lips that killed the taste of the most bitter liquor
and all the restless nights where I killed girls in your name*

*Hoping you would be one of them*

*Her wrists dripped such
beautiful paint for you to paint such masterpieces*

*don't say that her canvas wasn't good enough nor was she a
masterpiece*

*Poetic Alcoholic*

*I sat down, looked at her and wiped the tears
the ones that dripped from the wells of paradise*

*her universe was you now, she had abandoned the one her
mother taught to cherish*

*Poetic Alcoholic*

*She created her masterpiece with tranquillity and confidence. She stroked it in colours, lines and curves she couldn't have imagined.*

*Where her lonely nights became the muse to her outline and where her tears became the ink to her canvas.*

*But the agonised critics dissolved her hope with weary comments and put her in the courts of God; the one who was sold to the highest bidder*

*and her trial became one to remember for she gave God his highest place and went to create the greatest masterpiece of all.*

*Herself*

*Listen to her. She'll inspire you.*

*but inspiration from her was a toxic that ruined man one by one.*
*her canvas were ones who were broken and for the ones who weren't broken;*
*she found them in her bed where man would listen to her voice while she peeled their skin*

*and spewed her toxic in them until the thought of lust.*

*She was the glisten of a masterpiece that exposed my demons in ways I couldn't imagine*

*She exhaled her toxic*

*I inhaled so deeply to get indulged in my own demise*

*god was sold to the highest bidder*

*god became a system
where the poor became followers of that religion*

*and the rich became the church*

*Rain was fragile but she wasn't; she had become ill to the cold
she was nothing but drizzle that I protected myself from*

*she was acidic*

*I loved the way she cries; slowly yet painfully
every tear defined her agony*

*and I stood there watching her kill herself
to my pleasure was her death*

*to her unfortunate was my applause and smile*

*Her words spewed venom that poisoned me slowly*

*but I loved it,*
*she loved me deadly and I loved the feeling of being killed*

*Relationships weren't something that brought forth purpose to me*

*I was too busy stuck in places that only gave me temporary pleasure*

*I used to dream of nights that fulfilled my eyes
with such deception*

*such words you had no endearment of noticing my tears*

*my eyes that drowned in the blur of your missing outline on
the pillow case*

*Poetic Alcoholic*

*I should've told you that your lips stank
your hands reeked, and your body spewed venom*

*you were all what was forbidden by god*

*your tears streamed so heavy,
your eyes that held such burdens of unease*

*but yet you still gave him a chance to destroy you*

*your tears were fake, and you were empty*

*I'm sorry but I had nothing after her*

*the petals that were you tore and fell heavy with the tears of my unjust eyes*
*I'm here damaged with the feelings that are shallow and not mine*

*I gave that fool everything*

*Her lips drenched the life out of me*

*but I welcomed her nightmares that brought peace to my demons*

*I had heard the cry of remorse in your voice
begging me to tear you apart*

*you had overdosed to the feelings of his heart that was
drained*

*The way she cried; her tears spewed drops of honey that screamed in agony*

*and there was me; I loved her screams, her sorrowful soul that wanted help but I had nothing to offer but words that meant nothing*

*The tips of your fingers that lingered with poison; seamlessly filled my emptiness with pleasure that was so profound*

*She knew she loved broken things*

*I had found love; love which was going to destroy me but I loved the way she ripped me apart bit by bit.*

*Cheating was pigmented in your lips
in those eyes that fooled me twice*

*shame on me for believing that you would understand what love was.*

*I saw her as a person that would write my wrongs into rights
but I told her that she was something that gave me life*

*I kept calling her names but she told me I was sick and I was tired
maybe I was*

*but she was dripping milk from the pores of goodness
maybe she was nothing but an illusion to my lust*

*Poetic Alcoholic*

*the nights that I couldn't fall asleep; I laid down trying to turn the oxygen off*

*trying to open the healed wounds and picking the hairs that brought me to agony of the blood that seeped down my veins*

*the blood that tasted like hard sour liquor that reminded me of her; her who I thought was a rose that was everlasting*

*but that rose was one of Lucifer that held me ransom of her perfume; her sweet and sour smell that devoured me to my destruction*

*where I had been blind folded and where I laid with my wrists open till the angels came.*

*I love you*
*but love was an illusion that invited you to a place where*
*things became liquid*

*where words became literature that brought you peace*
*but love was a gift given from the gardens*

*but love was mixed by man and became a system that*
*bought and sold emotions*

*where love was given a label and it was given a time.*

*I love the way you beg for the taste of my lips even when I'm far away*

*you beg for the honey that drips from my lips*

*which are nothing but poison for you.*

*my bottle was my heaven*

*the white tiled floor was a reflection of my hell
and the drops of my cold blood hitting the floor told the
morbid silent story of my life*

*that brought me to my knees and made me one with the
purges of my demons*

*Poetic Alcoholic*

*Made with the fragile love of a mother's love
cultivated with such remorseful nights*

*And yet you throw away such love with his heavy grips*

*Pure and innocent; given love and time but time ran with me for a while and then it turned against me as I got older where the love evaporated and the innocence was lost. but time was never against me, I had made time an enemy but he was never an enemy he was a friend that brought me to paradise.*

*Poetic Alcoholic*

*I was given black and white colours*

*and was instructed to paint my life in colours but all I knew was what a sorrow was and what a morbid death looked like.*
*now tell me there's one more colour in between it all; grey.*

*life was bleak and tainted with three colours and the rest was a lie beauty was a factor that created sanity in minds of the lustful creatures.*

*all beauty was insanity that drove each other to provide for a sense of love, a direction that caused us to provide emotions and an emotion that vested madness in man.*

*our body were reverends, our thoughts burned like falsified masses, a beauty that was a blessing but was one of the deadliest sins to man*

*You were like a closed music box*

*closed tight with the notions of love, that scared you from opening up*
*where you hid all the musical beauty of your existence;*
*where you glowed*

*You had the capability to adhere to any soul, yet you tore yourself apart*

*She was filled with the milk of the clouds, cold yet endearing*
*waiting endlessly on the edge to feel your hands amongst her skin*

*she loved your lips on her neck where you grew on her soul*
*cinnamon coated kisses that still linger on me with her perfume*

*I never meant to hurt you, it was all a mistake*

*(the one you hold in your hands; she's really mine)*

*Its 5 am*

*the reach of your soul lingers on the wrong side of my love your whispers weep such weary clouds of falsified attraction*

*all the miles we lost to the rapid risk of betrayal*

*Poetic Alcoholic*

*The nights of weary pain pinned me to the skins of white walls*

*Where the void of silence locked me to the screams of your voice*

*And I stood here looking out the window pane looking at the drops of Eden falling on the streets that ran with your blood*

*on the day where you left it all and the day where you killed me from the mirrors of unparalleled agony*

*Poetic Alcoholic*

*All the matters were on the outside of your skin that filled me with pleasure*

*your beauty on the inside didn't matter, you were nothing but a stranger in bed to me*

*you didn't complete me; it was all lies; you were the face of pleasure that fulfilled my emptiness*

*and you thought love was between us but I told you love was nothing to me*

*Swapping the agony for pleasure I gave you secrets that you thought were scents of love*

*They were nothing but lustful thoughts that would destroy you one day*

*Don't try to find the closure that doesn't exist, from the start of seconds that gave you light to what we were but it was nothing but darkness*

*Love was a token handed down too many; a gift of Eden*

*but love became an auction for lust, greed and pleasure.
love was an emotion sold and bought where lies and
literature was sold to obtain feelings*

*and humans became slaves to dependency and love became a
label for profit*

*The scariest part was that I didn't realize all those times*
*I slept next to those strangers, the ones who captivated me*

*In the memories of all those rainy nights where you came to visit me*

*These were the first writings of my youth where I went forth and discovered my talents as a writer and as person who could sit down with you; understanding what you are. The early poems that would spark the name, "Poetic Alcoholic" a year later. I wouldn't say that these are works of art but just thoughts I would run on from the rivers of my mind to the canvas that was pigmented by my endless wandering mind. You'll see how 16/17-year-old me thought and how his words were so angry yet cultivated that the words actually stood for something. But, nonetheless I've taken enough of your time. One last thing, some of these poems in this part don't have names so I'd like for you to title them in how you understand these pieces of poetry and dm them to me on my gram. (My favourite poem from my earlier days is called "Eden" I'm very proud of that one) Cheers.*

---

## <u>HEAVEN GREW WEARY</u>

Heaven grew cold once, she was thrown down from the skies, her wings clipped for her sins that burned her walls like catholic confessions. She had found god, she had found him in the form of grains of sand, his lips were like tangerines and his beautiful colour coded speech, she had found the devil in his educated eyes. She had found a home. I had found her outside in the rain crying, just a lost star to my lost faith.

## SHE

*Her voice lingered through the lifeless bleak cold room, she used to call in the wintery days that stole my sleep at 3 am. Her beautiful voice that whispered at first with the giggles as if I couldn't hear her. She was filled with all the colours that an artist like me lusted for, her beauty stained my heart and seeped down my sleeves as she had pigmented herself onto my skin. She was art, she was the saying of, "she was never finished just abandoned." She wept the sorrows of being misused and not appreciated for what she was or what she could've been. But to me, she was a piece of art that had every sorrow of mine in colours that had me intoxicated. Her late nights became my amnesia, her whispers haunted my purges and over the sunrise she fell asleep on the phone; where I laid thinking of how it would be that if I forgot the world and held her myself. But not every painting becomes reality, that's when I learned not every story has a beautiful ending but she was a beautiful story waiting to happen.*

## *TOXIN DEATH*

*She sipped the cup filled with the poisons of the day that seamlessly gave her life but also killed her slowly yet in a way she loved that she was dying, the toxins that washed away down her dry weary throat. She had dreamt of something else on the streets for herself. He on the other hand who couldn't get his sleep at night, who wandered the streets to fulfil his lust for that something good which was her; he ached for her but he knew that since that one night he had picked her up, she was instantly a pill that made him relapse on all the lust he had for her, he had found his toy and something to release his misery upon. She hid in a shell; she had grown immune to her body not being a temple anymore; better she was a doll for many. She was sick and tired, she had realised that she wasn't fireproof to life like once she had thought when her mother held her her hands, but that was all gone, she laid there after the countless nights she killed herself on the cold streets that she had called home, but as she sipped her beauty away, she let her ink spew from her veins onto the crystal morbid floor that welcomed her death.*

*The rain drops that seep down from the drowsy sorrowful clouds that fill your existence in each drop that hits me with the pain of a million dreadful wounds that I acquired on the swings of the play-set where I first saw your sliver lining. As the clouds, you shaded me for all my wrongs and as the rain in my life, you spewed the acidic rains over the scars that hadn't healed. Now it was you, me and the purges that were dragging me down to the black flames of hell.*

*Poetic Alcoholic*

*it's 4:55 am and I write about you in a state where I'm fully intoxicated as I write this, they say when a being is fully intoxicated he starts to spill the truth that lurks in the walls of his mind, which seeps so fluidly down a canvas which is you. Looking at you, the way I painted you in the beauty of the night sky that gave your colours the outline of a beautiful creation which nonetheless you are. Which soon turned out to be a lifeless piece of lie that means nothing to the strokes of such keys that play melodies and tunes that have no meanings.*

## Poetic Alcoholic

*You grew on me from the moment your fingers intertwined with the silk fingers that I so loathed to make from sandpaper, no matter what I thought about you, I had seen the true meaning of home and I had grown to realise that when I talked you, you listened and you had become one with one with my memories. The retention of knowing you for a life time had been drawn as an outline that was one I always knew. Somehow back in my head I was told I was going to reunite with one figure that would give me a peace of mind the one I had killed along time ago thus you were a discovery that came to me a stroke at time leading up to a masterpiece which was and always will be you and when I go home; you're one that's holding her arms open and waiting for me to dissolve myself in one with you.*

*The sky who looks so greatly down at his beautiful reflection which he doesn't pay attention to the one loves he used to call the sea as she glisters his heavenly reflection but for that man who strides with his heavy lonesome steps contemplates back to where he first met his love, where he first saw her outline on the edge of the pier, now he stands there writing till the ink grows one with the colourless paper that some stories don't have happy endings but the masterpiece she was had all the glistening colours of the love that once the sky and the sea shared but which had died a sorrowful death.*

## HIM

The world is tilting to the direction of your sorrowful emotions of what you had put on display. But you soon realised that loving hurts, it was the only thing that was keeping you alive. The photograph you held of him was just a sorrowful memory that was fading away day by day where you felt the agony with each tick of the dreadful sixty seconds. But loving was the only thing you knew, you always told yourself it would get easier the more distant you grew from him, but every time you closed eyes; you heard the words that sent you to the purges of your own hell. Every page you wrote about him turned against you, it deprived you of the life you had left. But it was time for you to come home to the street where you first saw his outline, where you took your first shot of love. It was a long day anyways but its time for you to go to sleep in your bathtub, where you found your veins staggered opened dying the colour of the water as you had poured red wine over yourself. And you laid there waiting to be wasted into the ocean of sorrows, the water that you go called home.

## *EDEN*

*Perhaps God was planting on the banks of the rivers of Eden and while growing his colourful flowers; he planted the wrong seeds. In the time being, he left his garden amidst angels who wandered and fell in love with each of his beautiful creations. They stumbled across a flower growing amongst the corner where God had not attended, where the soil was lifeless, colourless and inhabitable. But in all that sorrowful mist; the angels noticed a beautiful vivid flower growing in the sorrows of unplanted Eden. The angels had questions, they rushed to God with wings made of livid white clouds that a human would call flawless cotton balls. They bowed in front of the creator and without the angels even moving their mouths about the gorgeous flower, God spoke with a soft tone such as a mothers stroke through her child's hair and said, "You ask about the flower that grows with such weary cause but holds all the life of my Eden, which the flower holds a piece of me, a piece of me that grows from the sorrowful ground, a place where it has triumphed all those who have dragged it down to its purges but it came out beautiful and everyone fell in love with my best creation, which the flower is a **women.***

*Her lips so lustful yet filled with taste of the rivers of Eden, her lips that made liquor taste like drops of syrup dripping down my throat. she was the beauty that hid away at the bottom of the bottle that I clearly never finished, she was the last drop of faith that I seamlessly forgot while reading the letters of God. she was the last gleam of the sunshine on the edge of the horizon that gave me hope for who I was and where I was hidden. I had grown immune to the demons of the night and I had forgotten who she was in the intoxication but she was a storm, she was the drizzle that beautifully touched my face; so warm and gentle. She had drenched me in one notion of her smile that came from a colour coded mouth, with her intellectual eyes that held paradise but she was a treasure, she was my oxidation without any need to kill myself more.*

*Poetic Alcoholic*

*I'd sit here for countless days clogged up on the most bitter alcohol and write about you; the one thing I want but can't have, where the evenings turn into cold solid nights where the nights never see the light of dawn and then at the end of the dark I lay on your lap holding your fingers which are brushes to my canvas and all I see is paradise but the night time fades into a unparalleled nightmare where you taint my love with the love of his lustful fingers that grab you in ways I never would have, his touch glistens you in a way where he poisons you for his sins. I know your heart won't be mine but I promise I have the time to help you find all the words, melodies and memories that will tell you no lies of the beauty that you hold, but as long as you lay in his arms my eyes will weep the sorrows of your outline. I heard about all the love you put into him for you found out it was all lost, all the miles you put into him and you were standing still, I grew to fall even more into your abyss but now I believe there is no time for me to go home. I never doubted a single ounce of love I had for you until I grew tired of you throwing yourself on to people who treated you like a whore, but maybe those miles that you put into him are the ones you deserve and you call out that you need a figure that will pull you out from your late nights and amnesia, but that chapter ended when you closed your eyes and finally drowned in a place where you didn't belong and I finally let go of your hand and let you drown forever.*

*maybe I was emotional when I wrote this but maybe I said too much, I pushed my luck when I was with you, you were a shot of toxic and I took it till the man in black knocked on my door and took my dirty liquor filled soul*

*Poetic Alcoholic*

*I used to call everyday, to spew my addicted toxins over the phone in hopes you would glisten back into my life. But the dial always rang with a bleak tone that defined my time as blank-less space but now I speak the words to monotone women who lifelessly speaks and says to leave a message which you'll never reply too. Now I narrow the meaningless words to you through a void that will never reach you. "I hope you find the fulfilment of the void which you eagerly figure out to fill with every thought of you."*

*In all the bitter things that were toxic for me, you were the sweetest of them all. Your soft delicate skin which lingered your perfume that haunted me in every way possible, the way my mind, my soul lusted for your outline. The way my inner demons screamed the noises and tears of our sorrowful relationship. And at the end of us was the few words that seeped out my dry sorrowful mouth: there were colours, there was a light from Eden when you were near me, life was a living paradise but now it's an unfinished story that has died with you*

*Poetic Alcoholic*

*she lays there with her so called lover, the droplets run down her smooth heaven filled face, but he forgets that a piece of art lays next to him*
*where I drown in my bed where she isn't present, I beg for her, for the taste of her lips, the touch of her skin against mine, but she lays there next to him, where the tears of heaven fall down the rivers of Eden which flow from eyes and on to nude sweet lips. She lays not knowing that I lay here holding on to her love.*

*I won't let you down.*

*You sat on that empty seat and lingered for my soul, a soul who had endless love to offer and could not be depleted. You lingered for a being who would love you forever, and you set forth the notion of making him fall for you. The being himself never doubted himself for loving you all the way but he doubted her for not loving him fully. The effortless relationship went forward and he began to realise that this love was tainted, he was a fool who couldn't see past your pretty face and the things you did to fake the love. When you looked your best, he couldn't resist to love you even more for being art, he soon knew that this art was deception and was tearing him apart piece by piece, so the fool stopped being a fool for you and quit his worst habit.* **Her**

---

*Fin of the youthful adventures of myself, now you'll see how I've grown since this as you move forward in my mind.*

*her lips are a fade of a pink lush sunset,*
*which has a gentle beautiful tone.*
*her eyes are the colour of the morning dawn,*
*which carries mystery waiting to be discovered*

*her voice is something distant, something I'll never have*

*You called late nights, saying your goodbyes
it was all broken hearts and beats of unjust torture*

*the flowers on your porch still blossom; their scent lingers
in your voice*

*Poetic Alcoholic*

*I had you entangled in my sheets
drenched in your heavy breaths*

*pretending to love your moans; with her still on my mind*

*I took you by the tongue; scratching you in ways you wanted
and more
and here I sat tearing your skin open to expose your heart
I didn't love you*

*you were a bet that I needed to win*

*She was in my bed; looking at me with eyes that held her soul and her innocence*
*I was here to take your innocence but instead I broke you*

*Your best friend fucked better in bed.*

*God I was in love with you.*
*Maybe I wasn't but all I wanted after you left was to destroy you*

*So you could never think about loving again.*

*What was your voice to me?*

*It was a miserable voice filled with agony that tainted me with your love*
*at the end, it was you laying there; stone cold with eyes pouring blood*

*waiting for me to cry.*

*Poetic Alcoholic*

*Those nights when its pouring
the drops of his voice bring you home
And the nights where you hear his laugh as a violin*

*you wanted to forget but you had indulged yourself in your greatest beauty*

*She was desperate to feel his fingers against her skin
her eyes that hid behind the everglades of her bitter love*

*I wanted to feel your breaths on my neck as they were
named after me*

*I want to drink till I make a big mistake.*
*I want to lose my virginity and feel infinity.*

*I want to feel wasted and suicidal*

*Poetic Alcoholic*

*I loved you*
*I flew to close to the sun trying to light you as my moon*

**But death was more beautiful than you**

*there were nights where I lingered so immensely
nights where I couldn't slumber*

*those were times where he was deep in your soul;
searching for your aura; as one of his victims*

*Yes, I broke girls*

*I loved breaking some of them. I broke them till they loathed for me and slowly I killed them more till they were dry of blood.*

*I created stone cold killers.*

*I came home after the funeral; looking for pieces of your hair*
*too bad the maidens came in and your essence was lost with the other black hairs*

*Ones that tainted my white sheets*

*Love me or love me not
You weren't meant for love;*

*just amusement and hate*

*Poetic Alcoholic*

*I don't think I ever loved you
Maybe it was more a dearly lust that made me feel whole*

*Then again, you were a mere filling and there were more like you to betray.*

*Poetic Alcoholic*

*It was the endless nights
where we glistened as beacons of hope to other beings*

*And we were sought out to be calls of others on lonely nights*

*This isn't the last time you've seen me*

*I will come back through his eyes, his lust and his hands that hurt you*

*I loved you, but now you're bleeding for him*

*Its like your eyes bleed honey
for my mouth lusted for your pain
It was sweet nectar of your agony
and your scent that fed me wholly*

*There was this pleasure I got from you*

*It wasn't love nor was it sexual*
*It was the pleasure of breaking your heart and putting it back together.*

*You were truly a fool*

*What happens when you cry?*

*My heart feels content and your tears that sweeten my mouth*

*I love the feeling of you spilling your blood for me*

*Your fingers outlined my soul*

*Until your hands laid waste to my love for you.*

*Poetic Alcoholic*

*You beat me blue and thought love came from you stopping me from loving others*

*You were wrong; they loved me for me*

*You loved me for my skin that you left marks on*

*You thought love came from places that grew with you as a child*

*But you never realised that love was a factor you had to learn not achieve*

*You were crafted so beautiful by the universe
until he gave you a label and ruined your flowers*

*you were nothing but an useful object*

*I could feel the lips that were agile to the lust of my lips
the way she flipped her pain by the shakiness in her tone*

*We had found each other, broken but it was a mistake*

*I want to take you by the tongue and seep your honey*

*Until you have nothing left but toxic kills man*

*Your throat ran heavy with honey that you saved up your entire life*

*Whereas he cut your veins open and drank while you died slowly*

"Why me?"

*You loved him so much*

*You couldn't stand him looking elsewhere*

*That night the sheets were pigmented with his dead love*

*you laid so quietly; the sheets stained with your blood
maybe if you scream loud enough, god will hear your
prayers*


*but then again; your demise was my greatest achievement.*

*I'm listening to all the conversations when you're asleep*

*but when you're awake; nothing seems to be right*

*somewhere out there; you chose someone else*

*I hope you know that I still sit here*

*waiting for your scent to kiss me like summer kisses autumn*

*I had seen such beauty in you*
*in places where you hid your scars*

*in places, he never loved*

*but I'll never be with you*

*I worshipped her in the bedroom
condemned to her raw purges*

*where I showed my soul, and you sharpened your nails
deeper in my skin*

*you're the colour of my blood*

*I don't care about your wounds*

*every inch of your skin is a holy grail*

*red imprinted lips; sun silk eyes*

*my heart is filled with your perfume*

*don't say a word; you are beautiful, yet temporary*

*Poetic Alcoholic*

*you loved breaking the petals of flowers*

*like autumn rain that fell so softly*

*my heart was sculpted by your tears*

*melody of the angels; your voice was
you were a smooth breeze of dark January nights where the
moon fell love with her sun*

*and me? you had me by the scent of your raw skin*

*you were on the other side of the horizon waiting for her*
*fragile voice to say hello*
*even the stars bleed in agony for you*

*I can still hear your heartbeat on the radio*

*surreal melodies that has bestowed man
lathered in honey that drives man insane
your skin that holds him ransom*

*he is drowning in your aura*

*written in sculptures of god*
*beauty was engraved in his skin*
*and her? she was fully blinded by his soul*

*glimpse of a sunset; molded by the light of Eden
where he sits, wasted on scents of your perfume*

*waiting for your voice to finally give him rest.*

*black hazy hair filled with her emotions*

*he held her captive by his lonesome eyes*

*and she was another prisoner of his beautiful demise*

*toxic kisses placed in such places*

*her screams brought him such pleasure*
*he had broken her in places that, she never fathomed*

*she dripped honey from her plum lips*
*filled his wells till he oozed your poison*
*he'll never forget the taste of your tongue*

*but every woman haunted him by your perfume*

*a goddess of torment*
*a voice that left me alone*
*maybe all you were good for; was the view*

*and I laid with you but with the thought of someone else*

*lost in your ember eyes*
*your tears tasted like sweet cinnamon*
*you were violins of a symphony*

*beautiful yet so destructive*

*I saw him; drenched in your memory
his eyes painted bloodshot with your lust.*

*I just woke up with a girl who looked like you*

*the way your lips caress god's scent*
*your voice that falls so swiftly on his skin and here I lay;*
*intoxicated in your eyes*

*my emotions have already pulled the trigger*

*tempered with lust*
*your heart was hollow given the sanity of angels, yet you had fallen*

*in the midst of paradise; god had grown weary of you*

*your lips that burned the agony of love*
*your whispers that left me ill*

*and these nights, you still stroll my lips*

*honey coated petals of unused flowers*

*you became his beautiful demise*

*and here he laid, looking at your sinful eyes*

*he became immune to condemned prayers*
*your body; a temple he slowly fell in love with*

*and his heart became ransom to your pleasure*

*and I had found scents of his lust on your lips*
*where you had lost your soul*
*and you remembered what your heartbeat sounded like*

*it sounded like something I used to feel*

*two hearts in an unfaithful paradise*
*you had opened your heart, poured it into his whiskey glass*

*and he sat, intoxicated with his heart bleeding*

*same red lips, tainted with false love*
*I loved the taste of you; so raw and ripe*

*what sort of deed did I condone to watch you break in my hands?*

*he was an intoxication to you*
*he kept you amidst the angels but he himself was drowning*

*you were in love and he was dying*

*you were used, tormented and plagued*
*god had set afire your embers*

*he could never abandon such a masterpiece*

*Poetic Alcoholic*

*the fragrance of your skin filled my hollow heart*
*you were a surreal melody, one that had no shallows*

*and every time you opened your mouth, you took my breath*

*your tears ran freely, rivers of Eden flooded*
*where the angels ran dull in agony*
*and god stood still with lost faith*

*he had broken you, drained you of paradise*

*he was your escape on a lonely night
his dark tainted soul that held you ransom
you were scared of love.*

*all he did was break you, you loved being broken*

*I was lost in your love*

*your tears had grown the most beautiful flowers but your eyes had burned out*

*I never meant to hurt you*

*I took you by tongue*
*embraced your scarred skin*
*where I was indulged in your honey*

*where you made him forget his sins*

*you loved the feeling of cheating in his eyes
it brought you the lust of the imprisoned*

*the way you cheated on him last night and all those other times*

*you were a faint rainy day memory*
*where the petals of lonesome flowers remorse your death*

*where my breath still tainted of your scent*

*you were paradise in forms of sand; I saw it in your eyes
your goodbye cut my veins*

*and me? I completely lost sense of reality*

*I miss you; you were my heart, dipped in gold, tore me apart;*
*a piece that took my aura*

*do you think of me once in a while*

*the way your tears fell from the stars*
*my fingers that clenched your skin fearing a goodbye*

*I knew then how fragile you were*

*I wanted to feel your blood on my fingers*
*I was drenched in fear of jealousy*

*after I was done all you were, was lifeless*

*silent nights I lay awake*
*your eyes that burn into my eyes like embers of hell*
*your honey that was toxic*

*my eyes bleed with regret, and you drown with agony*

*then again when I opened my eyes*
*I could taste your scent even when you loved me*
*I felt strayed maybe I was in love*

*you still linger in my heart*

*I have loved you since the day you ran your eyes across my soul*
*all those times, where I would dream of your body stitched to mine*

*I have realised that maybe you slept alone all those nights too*

*you were the sound of falling rain*
*I fell in love with into the winds*
*and the sunset that filled me with colours of his garden*

*filled with glistening petals of roses*
*she had filed my hollow heart with symphonies of chaos*
*I was intoxicated by her ember like eyes*

*I too want to feel paradise in her voice*

*The void that I filled with all those men in his thoughts*

*sleepless nights with the bruises on my skin that ached for home*

*his filth murdered me*

*I wanted to feel the sounds of your voice in the midst of my bleeding eyes*
*your sinful fingers that laid waste to my soul*

*I just wanted you to feel pain.*

*Poetic Alcoholic*

*I could taste the sour heartbreak
when you spoke, I fell deeper into my tears
my heart was broken, yours was being filled*

*all you ever did, was lie*

*Since you had left*
*I could hear the birds loath in your desire*

*and all I had left; was your laugh on voicemails*

*I'll always be watching in every smile you break*

*I wanted to wrap my hands around your neck*
*where your tears fuelled my agony*
*I listened to your screams*

*I too had fallen into distraught of you*

*drenched in your endless honey*
*where I was lost to the scents of your lust*
*your lips were destruction of wars*

*muses of my demise, you were; and I? was dead all along*

*I want to talk about your eyes*
*the ones who hold so much agony that weep through heavy*
*tears*
*I love the way you screamed at me; your voice that trembled*
*you were dying slowly, with the wells of paradise which ran*
*dry*

*you were gorgeous, now you're hollow; dead and fearful of*
*him and all other men who try to love you*

*I loved the way you cut open my skin
filled it the delicate flowers of his Eden
and kept me to the arms of your damaged skin*

*maybe love wasn't meant for people like me. I on the other hand always thought, my good character would resort in things being in line with her parents. But then again I had grown immune to all the factors of caring what others said about me. I had never known the feeling of being told, yeah you aren't like us nor do you have the money to compare to someone.*

*I recently have been kept away from all my notions of literature, its hard for me to sit down and let my thoughts transcend to this canvas. It's funny to me, people cry with such heavy tears that, "oh god they broke me but then they go running back into the same arms that keep burning their skin." As of right now, there is a constant state of war within myself. There are so many of you that endow me with your endless love. I always grew to love every single person that ever seeped my blood.*

*I crave her voice but yet I fear that my breaths that I fume are not enough for her thirst. "Hasan, its going to work out, always have faith." I hid behind the curtains of my eyes to seep out the devil that lives in my heart where I am lost in my dreams.*

*I ask you all, what does it feel to have a heartbeat?*

*It's like some took the beauty of paint in the tubes of honey of Eden. Let it spill all over the white canvas that held no hope, and with his tears of agony and love; you emerged with your colours that entitled him the glory of god's grace*

*For @maiarabbas*

*I still remember the taste of your lips*
*even when I saw his eyes wrapped up around your soul*
*you were indulged in his toxic, blindly*

*you were captive of his lust that eagerly destroyed you*

*the way her eyes glazed the edge of paradise*
*her plum filled lips that held warm blood that I wanted to feast on*

*I was ransom to her literature and her skin that I wanted to make home.*

*I had found you in the midst of my intoxication
your eyes gave me the glimpse of paradise
I had become immune to the cradles of your hair that
devoured me*

*you were my eternity, my end to the fragrance of god's
garden*

*I wanted to wrap my hands around her neck
suffocating her demons with my intoxication
her honey spewed all over my mouth
with the sheets that pigmented god's cologne.*

*she breathed harder, I fell deeper into her abyss*

*today, I smelled your perfume in my coat*
*lingering in my hair with your soul hanging to my waist*
*your eyes held the embers that tore you apart*

*your silenced lips gave me your tears*

*every time you hurt him the more he cries*
*with your ill fragrance all over his sheets*
*cold without your soul, your voice that left him with those*
*tears of remorse*

*every time he closes his eyes; your lying lips tear him apart*

*the imprisonment of me with the outline of your lips*
*how you tore me apart with the stings of saturated hate*
*I don't want to die in your tainted sheets*

*listen, your voice still lingers in my hollow mind*

*I think about your scent that taught me how to live
you were the sound of drizzle that fell so quietly
glistening of a sunset that hid my ocean of tears*

*I stood in the chaos of the pain of your lips on his*

*the velvet glazed taste around her thighs attracting strangers*
*she was raw, an injection of a film that brought man such insanity*
*a surreal melodies of moans that tempted murders of souls*

*at the end, she was floating in her own pool of blood.*

*you reminded me of a cold winter breeze*
*filled with the scents of weary nights*

*with your skin that held my soul so gently*

*winter was gone and had died with you*

*petals of flowers spewed out her mouth*
*ones that held me by the tongue*
*her perfume that tainted my lingering soul*

*she was the sunset in my eyes; perfect disaster to my demise*

*It's like someone took the tone of your skin and lurked it into pieces of glass that held blades to my soul that bled so heavy for you. Your skin which was a holy grail that my heart has been intoxicated by; your breaths that lean upon my filthy skin. You are filled with Eden and I am here, in your sheets; waiting to be consumed*

*why do you torment me?*

*your tears were like acid rain that corroded my skin*
*I had lost all glory of love in your broken heart*
*the world was falling, you had lost grip of reality too*

*all these melodies of pigmented love had been murdered.*

*My hands down your spine, pigmenting you from your lips
Your innocence in the palm of my hands*

*asking to be damaged.*

*Poetic Alcoholic*

*I had tried to deny every tear I let out for you
all the time, I've wasted in your sad presence*

*I hadn't been enough, with you tearing us apart*

*I miss the warmth of December
the smell of your skin and the whispers of your laugh*

*You still exist in my life through my closed eyes and my helpless dreams*

*I remember the scent of your hair with the voices of symphonies of violins*

*I can remember the taste of your lips in the enclaves of my mouth heaven was your smile with the oceans drowning me in your soul.*

*Its not that I wanted to leave*
*I just got tired of searching for you*

*You were the reason the sky cried in agony; which wept in gloom*
*for the slow pain of the clouds was your lonesome days*

*It was your eyes that bled empathy*

*But my mouth drooled toxic, losing opportunity*

*Salivating that either of us mattered to reality*

*I still think about your blue eyes
the ones that drowned me*

*and broke every vow.*

*Poetic Alcoholic*

*You were the glistening pillars in my palace
and every time I closed my eyes
I could smell your sweet presence*

*the walls seep of your honey in my head which is all ruins.*

*Its like her lips spewed such immense toxic
all I wanted was to find her purges of ends*

*I drowned myself in her silkily skin; and I lost myself.*

*Her body melted with such hate that her lust was all
but your vessel of faith*

*She was a temple before you; even you had laid waste to god;
such deliberate destruction of creation that begged mercy.*

*You were creases of a time that had no middle*
*your voice grew with your lies*
*at the end, your eyes that ran with thick mascara that*
*pigmented how death loved to see you swim*

*in your own demise.*

*Poetic Alcoholic*

*Torn apart by the ones that hoped tranquility
they killed me; the ones who are to help blossom are the
ones that count your petals*

*unjust beauty and suck your nectar unjustly
from your throat to give you death, that even death bleeds*

*day and night*
*your sweet voice that spews such love*

*yet I still linger for something sweet*

*to me it was an unholy way to save my blood*
*to others, I was a tainted person*

*screams and blood gave my family hope*
*but it gave the world a reason to fear the mask I wore*

*My heart which overflows with your uncertain perfume
That makes me wonder; why your sheets are half empty on
days of such delight*

*Sometimes, I pick up the phone and I hear your voice that
looked for the goodness in*

*my lustful eyes*

*You were a storm that let the petals of flowers live calling the drops of your honey that agonised every ounce of your blood*

*that bled so heavily from your hungry eyes*

*I hope I never be a burden; swim with me please, I can almost see the beach*

*Poetic Alcoholic*

*Then there's you
filled with all the false aura of false gods
your mouth that seeps such heavy poison scripts*

*all you hold is anger of someone you aren't; carbonated,
filled with the toxic of sin*

*your body loops in relapse of the sunrise you'll never be; a
horrendous disaster you were.*

*Poetic Alcoholic*

*Her soft oceanic eyes that held the blue mist of the colours of my blood
she spewed nectar from her mouth that embarked her lips with the taste of Eden*

*she was the drizzle in the midst of all chaos; slowly that intoxicates and all at once*

*You have to realise that she loves dancing, with the flowers in her hair*
*with her perfume that lingers on the edges of her lips*

*but times get old, she hates to dance and the flowers that cultivated her are no longer in alive*

*now she hates to dance and you no longer feel her in your heart*

*Silence of the chance of love*
*nectars of desired prayers*

*where you hide in the rivers of my heart*
*petals of such delicate romance*

*I loath to drink the sweetness off your saturated lips*

*Sometimes I feel like you'll walk through that door
but you never seemed to be home*

*clearly you were breaking and I am too; all the way*

*Poetic Alcoholic*

*You could hear her begging in her tears*
*All the times I wanted to wander your mind*

*In all, you were just violence in all the hands that belonged*

*All those nights you slept drying your eyes*
*those heavy burdens that you yelled upon your wrists*

*you had lost yourself to the blood loss of the storm you once were*

*He had called you beautiful
you thought the way he touched your canvas
the way he scratched your skin and bit your neck
when he held you down and you thought it was love*

*when he whispered, "you're the best I had"*

*you were entitled to more than his "love" but you didn't
realise your self worth*

After reading this book to myself and looking at the direction of everything in my life, I'd like to take this moment and thank everyone who helped me create and reach this point, who have pushed me to be the best I could have been. Everyone in my life I've met, no matter who, has inspired me to create at some point. From the coffee runs at 6 am to the late night bar dinners to the travels across this globe has helped to create this piece of literature to showcase in ways who I am. Thank you for believing in me, this is a start to something beautiful with every single one of you.

With this being said, I hope the notions of my creations held onto you in ways you never thought they would and pushed you to realise where sadness and happiness lays in yourself and one another. You have been filled with the goodness in all that exists and you are the sole reason for you to be beautiful, because without you, there is no beauty. The pain exists and causes the torment, I know trust me. But we push and we strive to become the better of what we are and strive to learn that knowledge does not come from once source, it comes from every living thing. I know we all fall and make mistakes but don't let that stop you from bettering yourself and don't take that as a failure; push until you are where you want to be. Failure is another opportunity to another door in life. Don't take yourself for someone not valuable, you hold value and intelligence that holds such glory to such extent that you bring such melody to mankind. You are worth everything to someone who has been blessed to see you as a blessing, we aren't made to glow in front of everyone's eyes or mind. Some people don't have the eyes to see you as blessing thus don't put in effort into someone who isn't worth your time.

*To new beautiful beginnings with you and I together where life takes us; what new literature and gifts there are to come. Thank you for taking your time and patience in reading, understanding what "Poetic Alcoholic" was.*

*All the love,*

*Hasan*

*Poetic Alcoholic*

www.ingramcontent.com/pod-product-compliance
Lightning Source LLC
Chambersburg PA
CBHW032036290426
44110CB00012B/830